MEGA-COOL
MEGAFAUNA
Creatures of Ancient Lands

Anastasia Suen

Before Reading: *Building Background Knowledge and Vocabulary*

Building background knowledge can help children process new information and build upon what they already know. Before reading a book, it is important to tap into what children already know about the topic. This will help them develop their vocabulary and increase their reading comprehension.

Questions and Activities to Build Background Knowledge:

1. Look at the front cover of the book and read the title. What do you think this book will be about?
2. What do you already know about this topic?
3. Take a book walk and skim the pages. Look at the table of contents, photographs, captions, and bold words. Did these text features give you any information or predictions about what you will read in this book?

Vocabulary: *Vocabulary Is Key to Reading Comprehension*

Use the following directions to prompt a conversation about each word.

- Read the vocabulary words.
- What comes to mind when you see each word?
- What do you think each word means?

Vocabulary Words:

- carnivores
- cycads
- dromaeosaurid
- fossils
- hadrosaur
- herbivores
- megafauna
- omnivores
- ornithomimid
- scythe

During Reading: *Reading for Meaning and Understanding*

To achieve deep comprehension of a book, children are encouraged to use close reading strategies. During reading, it is important to have children stop and make connections. These connections result in deeper analysis and understanding of a book.

 ## Close Reading a Text

During reading, have children stop and talk about the following:

- Any confusing parts
- Any unknown words
- Text to text, text to self, text to world connections
- The main idea in each chapter or heading

Encourage children to use context clues to determine the meaning of any unknown words. These strategies will help children learn to analyze the text more thoroughly as they read.

When you are finished reading this book, turn to the next-to-last page for **Text-Dependent Questions** and an **Extension Activity**.

Table of Contents

The Ancient Lands 4

Herbivores of the Ancient Lands 10

Carnivores of the Ancient Lands 18

Omnivores of the Ancient Lands 22

Finding More 28

Glossary 30

Index 31

Text-Dependent Questions 31

Extension Activity 31

About the Author 32

The Ancient Lands

Was there once a turtle with claws three feet (one meter) long? That's what scientists thought when they discovered

these **fossils**. They named it *Therizinosaurus*, the "**scythe** lizard." Then, more fossils were found. Scientists thought they were dealing with a sea creature, but the truth was different. This was **megafauna** that lived on land! It was a dinosaur that was over 25 feet (7.6 meters) long and weighed more than 10,000 pounds (4,536 kilograms)!

This fossilized Therizinosaurus egg is about 70 million years old.

Don't Eat Me!

Therizinosaurus *had a small head and teeth just right for eating plants. It didn't use its long claws to catch prey. Instead, Therizinosaurus used its claws to fight back when other animals tried to eat it.*

Creatures lived on land long ago when there was only one continent named Pangaea. It had one sea around it named Panthalassa. As time passed, the land moved and broke apart to form the seven continents that we know today. The bodies of water around these continents have been given five different names depending on where they are located.

Pangaea

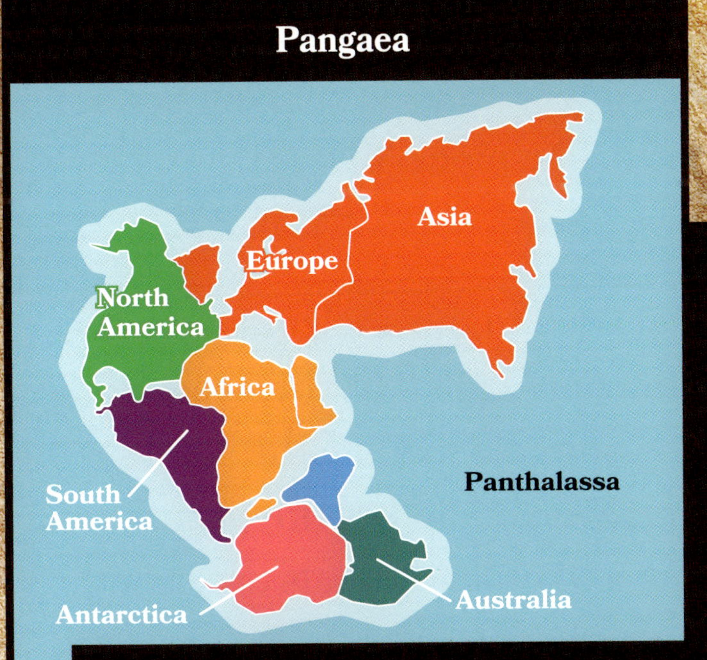

From One Ocean to Five

The Pacific Ocean, the Atlantic Ocean, the Arctic Ocean, and the Indian Ocean are the oldest named oceans. In 2000, the Southern Ocean (circling Antarctica) was named by the International Hydrographic Organization.

The World Today

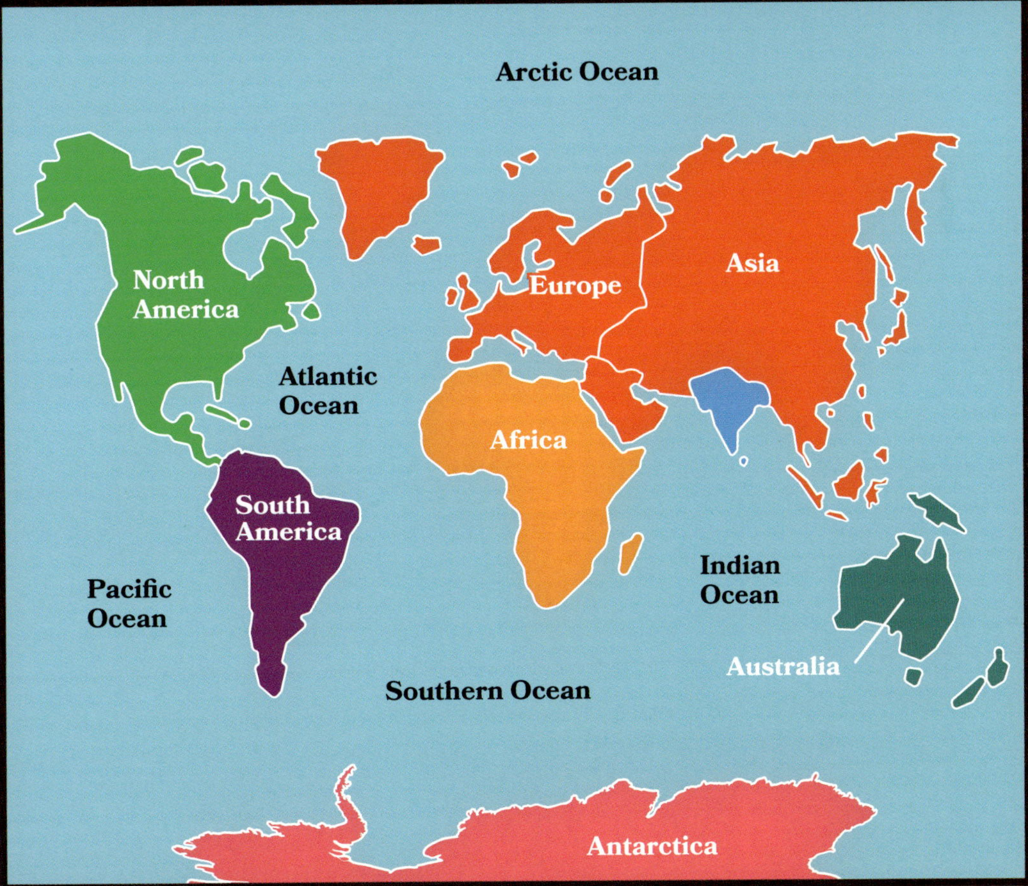

During the Mesozoic Era, ferns grew around short, stubby trees called **cycads**. Gingko trees grew even taller. There were also conifer trees, like pines, that grew seeds inside of cones.

Most of the creatures that lived in the ancient lands ate plants. Animals that eat plants are called **herbivores**. Some ancient land animals ate the animals that ate the plants. Animals that eat other animals are called **carnivores**. Animals that eat both plants and other animals are called **omnivores**.

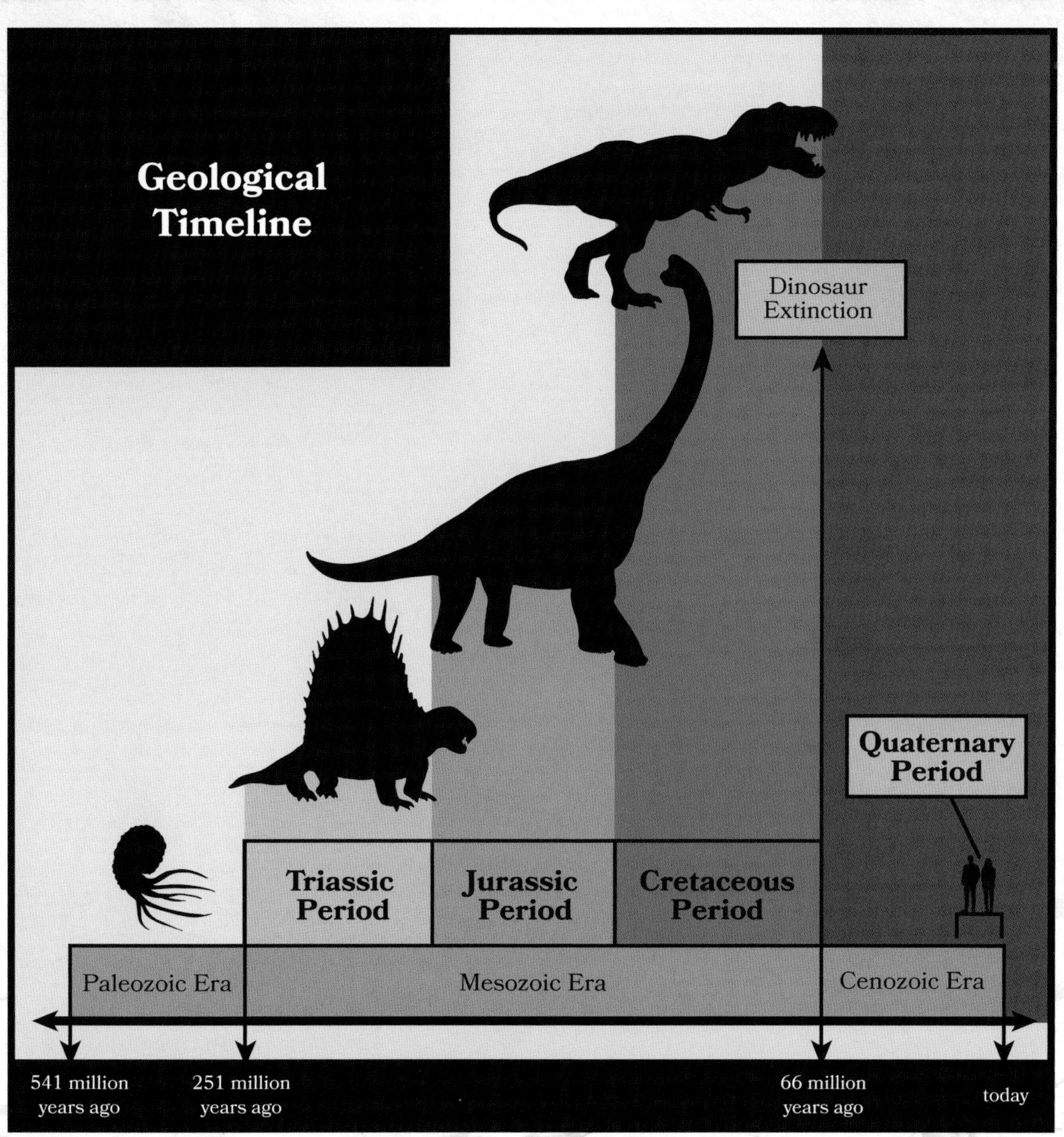

You live in the Quaternary Period of the Cenozoic Era. The creatures of the ancient lands lived during the Mesozoic Era.

Herbivores of the Ancient Lands

Patagotitan, found in Argentina in 2014, could be the biggest dinosaur to ever walk the Earth. It was a sauropod, a large dinosaur with a long neck and a long tail that walked with all four thick legs. Scientists say this dinosaur was more than 120 feet (36.5 meters) long and probably weighed more than 14,000 pounds (6350 kilograms).

Scientists categorize living things in many different ways. A single living thing can fit into more than one category. The very last sauropods alive were the largest ones, and scientists have another name for them: titanosaurs.

Triceratops, such as the one in this model, was an herbivore.

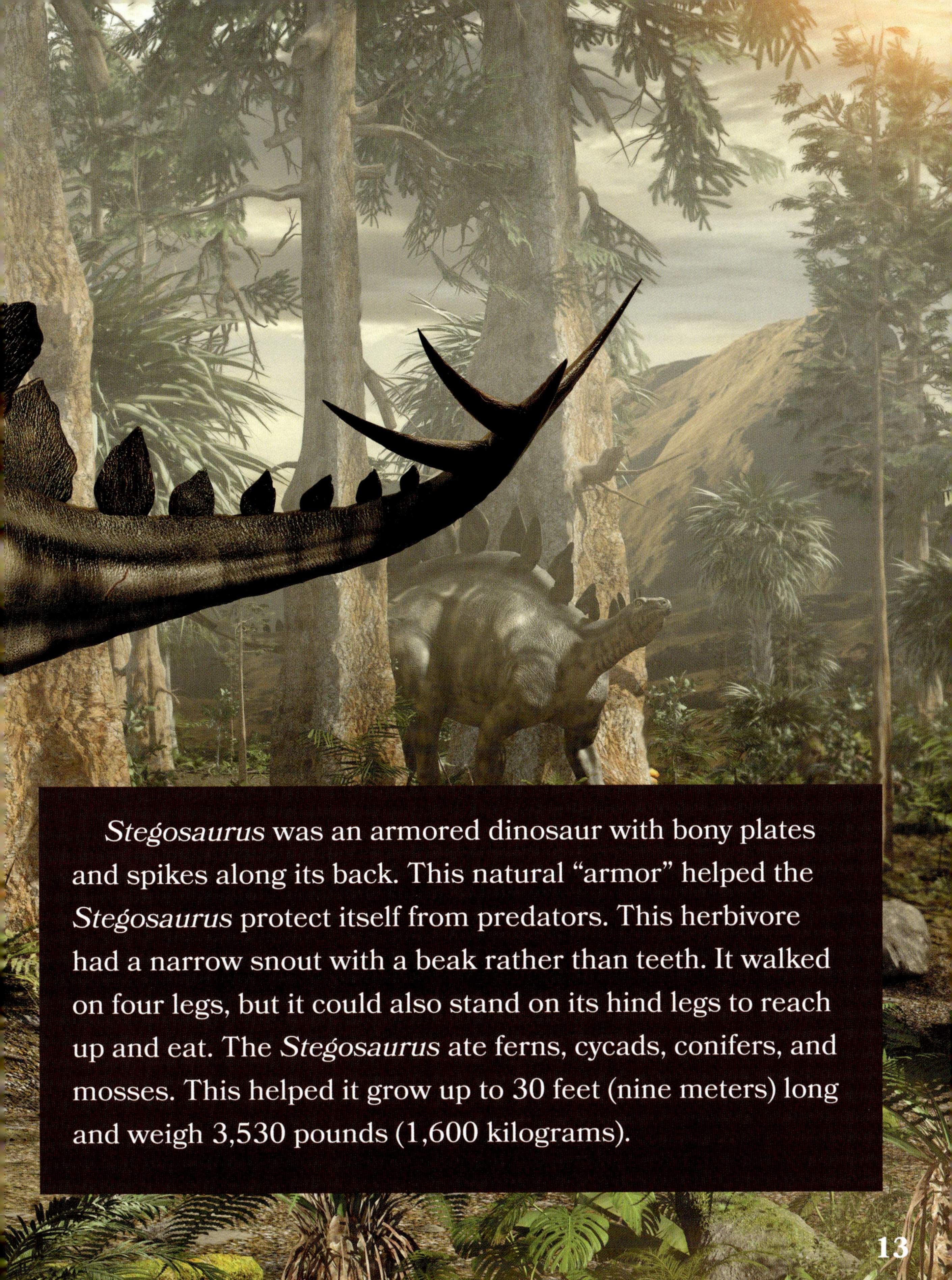

Stegosaurus was an armored dinosaur with bony plates and spikes along its back. This natural "armor" helped the *Stegosaurus* protect itself from predators. This herbivore had a narrow snout with a beak rather than teeth. It walked on four legs, but it could also stand on its hind legs to reach up and eat. The *Stegosaurus* ate ferns, cycads, conifers, and mosses. This helped it grow up to 30 feet (nine meters) long and weigh 3,530 pounds (1,600 kilograms).

When a horn fossil was discovered in the state of Colorado in 1888, scientists thought it was a bison. The next year, an entire skull with three horns was found. Scientists realized it was a dinosaur and named it *Triceratops*, or "three-horned face."

A *Triceratops* could have 800 teeth at one time. Scientists think it ate ferns, cycads, and palms. This dinosaur walked on four legs and grew up to 30 feet (nine meters) long. A large *Triceratops* could weigh 15,750 pounds (7,150 kilograms).

A Big Head

*At 10.5 feet (3.2 meters)
high,* Pentaceratops *holds
the Guinness World Record
for the largest land animal
skull ever found. You can see
this "five-horned face" skull
at Oklahoma's Museum of
Natural History.*

Magnapaulia was a **hadrosaur**, a duck-billed dinosaur. Found in Mexico, it was 50 feet (15 meters) long and weighed 25 tons! With its long bill, this dinosaur ate plants near the water. *Magnapaulia* also had a large hollow crest in its skull. When it breathed in, the air went up and around many times inside the crest. Scientists think the crest helped hadrosaurs make loud, deep sounds.

It took years to dig up a *Tyrannosaurus rex* (also called a *T. rex*) in Canada. Why? It was 42 feet (12.8 meters) long and weighed 19,555 pounds (8,870 kilograms). *Tyrannosaurus rex* means "king of the tyrant lizards." The scientists gave it the nickname "Scotty." Also known as "The King of Dinosaurs," *T. rex* was a theropod, a "beast-footed" dinosaur that walked on two legs.

Who is the Biggest *T. rex*?
In 1991, scientists said that Scotty was the biggest T. rex ever found. However, they only found 65 percent of Scotty's fossils. The biggest T. rex skeleton before Scotty was 90 percent complete. Which dinosaur do you think was bigger?

Utahraptor is the largest of all raptor dinosaurs. It had a large, curving claw on each hind foot that was almost 12 inches (30 centimeters) long. A *Utahraptor* could grow to 25 feet (7.62 meters) long and weigh almost a ton. *Utahraptor* is also the oldest known **dromaeosaurid**.

Like modern birds, dromaeosaurids were theropods with two legs and claws that grab. Scientists say they are both maniraptors, creatures with "seizing hands." Just like raptor birds, *Utahraptor* used its claws to eat the animals it caught.

Killed with One Kick!
Scientists think that Utahraptor *could kill another dinosaur with just one kick. When it extended a claw on its hind foot,* Utahraptor *could slice open a cut five feet (1.5 meters) long in its prey!*

In 1965, scientists in Mongolia found two fossil arms that were almost eight feet (two meters) long. The three fingers on each hand had claws that were eight inches (20 centimeters) long. Scientists thought they had found a new theropod dinosaur. They named it *Deinocheirus*, which means "terrible hand."

More fossils were found in 2013. *Deinocheirus* wasn't a theropod. It was an **ornithomimid**, a "bird mimic" that weighed between seven and ten tons! It was 16 feet (five meters) tall and more than 33 feet (ten meters) long with a sail on its back.

Stomach Stones

One of the Deinocheirus specimens found in 2013 had 1,100 gastroliths inside. These are stones that animals swallow to help them grind up plants they eat. There were also fish scales inside its stomach. This information helped scientists learn that Deinocheirus was an omnivore.

Gigantoraptor was an oviraptorosaur, a 3,086-pound (1,400-kilogram) dinosaur that ran on two legs. This dinosaur was 26 feet (about eight meters) long and was discovered in 2005, when scientists found a nearly complete *Gigantoraptor* fossil specimen in Mongolia. It had long sharp claws and a sharp toothless beak that could crush seeds, nuts, and even bones!

For years, scientists thought that *Pachycephalosaurus* was a plant eater. Their fossils had large rib cages, which was common in herbivores. Then, in 2018, scientists found a young *Pachycephalosaurus* skull in the state of Montana with flat teeth in the back and sharp teeth in the front. Scientists think that young *Pachycephalosaurus* might have eaten ferns and bushes as well as frogs, salamanders, lizards, small mammals, and other dinosaurs. That might have helped them grow up to 15 feet (4.5 meters) long.

Who Are You?

Scientists gave dome-headed dinosaurs different names based on the shape of their skulls. Now, some scientists think these skulls changed as the dinosaurs grew, so young dinosaurs looked different from adults. Could Dracorex *and* Stygimoloch *fossils really be the fossils of young* Pachycephalosaurus *instead? Only more research will tell.*

Finding More

Fossils are all we have left of these ancient land creatures. Scientists are always looking for more. Each new discovery helps scientists see the fossils they already have in new ways.

1. *Therizinosaurus*: 25 feet (7.6 meters) long
2. *Patagotitan*: 120 feet (36.5 meters) long
3. *Stegosaurus*: 30 feet (nine meters) long
4. *Triceratops*: 30 feet (nine meters) long
5. *Magnapaulia*: 50 feet (15 meters) long
6. *Tyrannosaurus rex*: 42 feet (12.8 meters) long
7. *Utahraptor*: 25 feet (7.6 meters) long
8. *Deinocheirus*: 33 feet (ten meters) long
9. *Gigantoraptor*: 26 feet (eight meters) long
10. *Pachycephalosaurus*: 15 feet (4.5 meters) long

Glossary

carnivores (KAHR-nuh-vawrs): animals that eat only other animals

cycads (SAHY-kads): plants with a thick trunk and leaves on top

dromaeosaurid (DRO-me-uh-SAWR-id): a family of theropod dinosaurs that lived in the Jurassic and Cretaceous periods

fossils (FOS-uhls): remains, impressions, or traces of a living thing from a former geologic age, such as a skeleton or footprint

hadrosaur (HAD-ruh-sawr): a dinosaur that walked on two legs with broad, flat jaws for scooping up water plants

herbivores (HUR-buh-vawrs): animals that eat only plants

megafauna (MEG-uh-faw-nuh): giant animals

omnivores (OM-nuh-vawrs): animals that eat both plants and other animals

ornithomimid (or-nith-uh-MY-mid): a dinosaur with extremely long limbs and neck that walked on two legs

scythe (siTHe): a tool with a large blade used for cutting

Index

Deinocheirus 22, 23, 29

Gigantoraptor 24, 25, 29

Magnapaulia 16, 17, 29

Pachycephalosaurus 26, 27, 29

Patagotitan 10, 11, 29

Stegosaurus 12, 13, 29

Therizinosaurus 4, 5, 29

Triceratops 11, 14, 15, 29

Tyrannosaurus rex 18, 19, 29

Utahraptor 20, 21, 29

Text-Dependent Questions

1. How do we know that megafauna lived long ago?

2. How do scientists figure out the size of a dinosaur?

3. What is another name for theropods with two legs and claws that grab?

4. Why did scientists change the names of some of these ancient land animals?

5. Most of the creatures that lived in the ancient lands ate plants. Why do you think this was the case?

Extension Activity

Make a diorama for an ancient land animal. Include one source of food. Decide if you want to show the creature eating or looking for food in its natural environment.

About the Author

Anastasia Suen is the author of more than 350 books for children, teens, and adults. She lives in the foothills of Northern California, which was underwater when dinosaurs were alive.

www.rourkeeducationalmedia.com

PHOTO CREDITS: cover: Shutterstock / GettyImages; page 3: Shutterstock; page 4: Wikimedia Commons / Woudloper / RG5 / WENN / Newscom; page 5: Shutterstock; page 6: GettyImages; page 7: Shutterstock; page 8: Shutterstock; page 10: Shutterstock; page 11: GettyImages / © Artush; page 12-13: Shutterstock; page 14: GettyImages / © MR1805; page 15: GettyImages / Orla / Shutterstock; page 16-17: GettyImages / Warpaintcobra; page 18: GettyImages / Orla; page 19: Callum Moffat / Daily Record / Newscom; pages 20-21: Shutterstock; page 22: Album / Prisma / Newscom; pages 23-27: Shutterstock; page 28: GettyImages / © AlenaPaulus

Edited by: Tracie Santos
Cover and interior design by: Lynne Schwaner

Library of Congress PCN Data

Creatures of Ancient Lands / Anastasia Suen
(Mega-Cool Megafauna)
ISBN 978-1-73164-350-6 (hard cover)(alk. paper)
ISBN 978-1-73164-314-8 (soft cover)
ISBN 978-1-73164-382-7 (e-Book)
ISBN 978-1-73164-414-5 (ePub)
Library of Congress Control Number: 2020945085

Rourke Educational Media
Printed in the United States of America
01-3502011937